S0-ASB-934

SECRETS OF
A CYPRESS SWAMP

SECRETS OF
A CYPRESS SWAMP

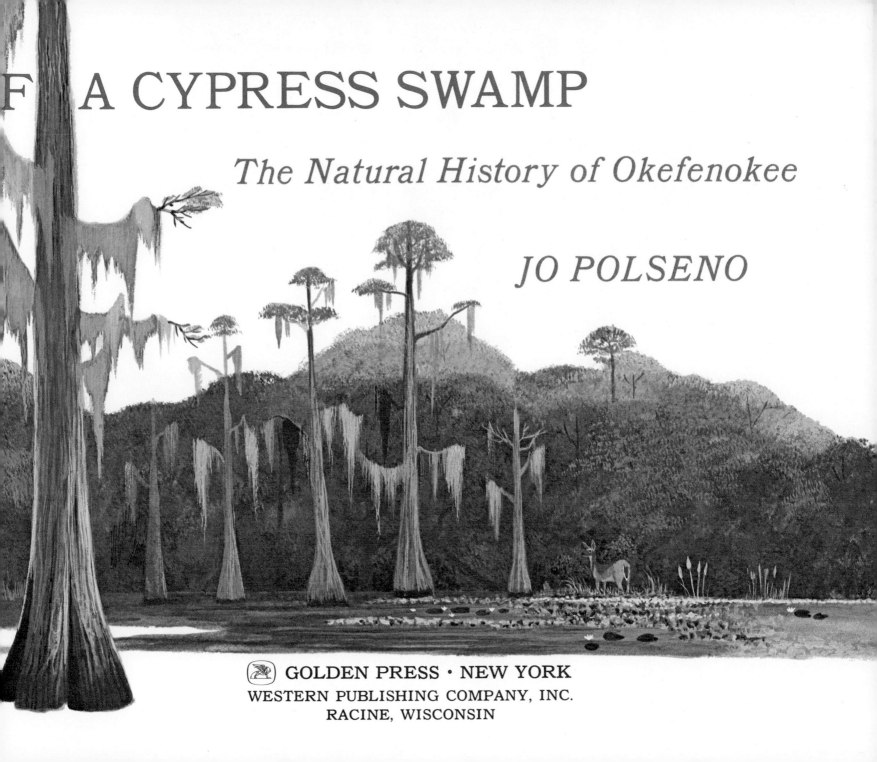

F A CYPRESS SWAMP

The Natural History of Okefenokee

JO POLSENO

GOLDEN PRESS · NEW YORK
WESTERN PUBLISHING COMPANY, INC.
RACINE, WISCONSIN

Copyright © 1976 by Western Publishing Company, Inc. All rights reserved. Printed in the U.S.A.
Golden, A Golden Book®, and Golden Press® are trademarks of Western Publishing Company, Inc.
Library of Congress Catalog Card Number: 75-24671

In southern Georgia, south of Waycross and north of Fargo, there is a swamp that stands forever in the glow of an eternal twilight beneath a canopy of bearded cypress giants. There is no sound except that of the copper-colored water as it swirls past the trunks of the ancient cypress trees, adorned with garlands of Spanish moss. The sun-dappled water and the deep-shadowed moss camouflage the hiding places of the wild creatures that prowl by day and of the hunted ones that flee into the darkness.

As silently as a falling leaf, a young doe and her fawn appear at the water's edge. The morning hush is broken by the call of a cardinal as a mockingbird sings from a loblolly bay—the first sounds to drift through the mist of the dark and mysterious Okefenokee Swamp.

It is a moment in the early morning glow just before moonset. A barred owl hoots in the stillness of the half-light. Deep from within the swamp comes the faint and distant answer of another owl, a double lament to a disappearing moon. A chuck-will's-widow makes her last lonely call. There is no answer and suddenly the moon is gone.

With the dawn come the sounds of the awakening swamp. Fish crows stir in their roosts while catbirds "mew" from the honeysuckle. A huge alligator rises to the surface of the dark-brown water and drifts slowly, like a floating log, to the center of the channel. A marsh rabbit swims quickly to the safety of the opposite shore.

From his lookout post on the limb of a black gum tree, a solitary wood stork stares down at the world of Okefenokee. An ordinary day in an extraordinary swamp has begun.

Deep in the center of Okefenokee's dark waters springs the source of the ever-winding and graceful Suwannee River. From Big Water to the Sill, the Suwannee meanders through an enchanted forest of shrouded cypress trees from which come strange sounds that will haunt, forbid and yet beckon the curious intruder.

Hundreds of alligators bask in the rising sun; reflections shimmer in the quiet depths of Minnie's Lake. The ivory-billed woodpecker, last seen here many years ago, is gone now forever. Is it foolish to hope that

somewhere in the wilds of this primitive refuge the forest will echo once again with the loud hammering of this enormous bird? The ghost of the Carolina parakeet still flits through the Spanish moss, its screech lost in the rustle of a soft wind.

Yet, time has not changed all things. The white ibises still fly up river to their morning fishing grounds, just as they did a thousand years ago. The bellow of an alligator can still hush the swamp, and the little blue heron still preens in the misty shafts of the morning sun.

A flock of snow-white birds flutters down from the tops of the river cypresses and lands with delicate grace on the sunny side of the channel. The birds fluff and ruffle their feathers as the sun climbs higher in the sky. The beauty of their long aigrette plumes almost led to their extinction, but the hand of man, which can so easily destroy, lifted a pen and passed a law that put an end to the ruthless slaughter of these fragile birds.

Protected, the snowy egret regained its stature as a common bird, thanks to the action of the National Audubon Society and to the rangers who patrol the swamps of the Deep South.

Finally, the sun clears the tops of the river cypresses, beaming light and warmth into the shadowy recesses. The egrets are joined by white ibises and young little blue herons, and together these gleaming white birds dazzle the eye as they bask innocently and fearlessly in full sunlight.

Neverwets and water lilies cluster near the muddy banks on the opposite shore. Last year's marsh grasses lie twisted, brown and bent, and new green shoots of maidencane rise from the centers of the dead clumps.

The shadow of a large bird in flight races across the dark waters of the swamp and a loud, trumpetlike sound comes from the sky. The sound, the shadow and the bird become one as a huge wood stork lands clumsily among the lily pads. He is quickly joined by another, their glossy green heads glistening in the southern sun. Ironheads, the swamp people call them.

Soon the storks will build large rookeries of dead branches and debris, and Okefenokee will resound with the squawks of the newly hatched young birds.

Suddenly, the wood storks spread their huge wings and take to the treetops, there to become the silent sentinels of the awakening swamp.

17

Now you see her, now you don't. A female pied-billed grebe bobs up and down in the pickerelweed. Some call her the water witch, she disappears so quickly. Only her head shows as she swims. In a flash she is gone, then suddenly pops up thirty yards away.

Her floating nest is made of reeds and dried leaves, but the bed in which she lays her eggs is soft with the down she plucks from her own breast. When the time comes for her chicks to leave the nest, she will carry them "piggyback" until they can take care of themselves. They hide in the quiet coves where the pickerelweed and lily pads grow thick. The water witch and her brood feed on the tiny fish that dart through the channel grass.

A rustle in the reeds on the edge of the shore sends all the chicks dashing to their mother's side. She promptly tucks them under her wings and dives to the bottom of the cove.

A pale yellow sun burns its way through a hazy white sky. A strange-looking bird with a snakelike neck perches on the limb of a dead river cypress. His wings are outstretched, as if he is waiting for the first morning breeze to lift him, like a kite, into the sky. Actually, the anhinga is waiting for his wings to dry. If he were to dive into the water with his wings soaking wet, he would sink to the bottom like a stone. Most waterfowl have oil ducts that help them shed water but the anhinga has none.

The anhinga spends as much time drying his wings in the sun as he does submerged in the water. When his feathers are perfectly dry, he can dart after fish with the speed of an arrow.

Soon the river mist will rise to the warming sun, and the morning breeze will send tiny ripples across the water. The anhinga's wings are almost dry as he turns to face the sun.

Something large and heavy crashes through the bushes. It seems to care nothing for safety—this animal that has no regard for caution or for the art of silent lurking. There is only one animal in Okefenokee that runs, splashes and swims with such wild abandon and joy, and it is the fun-loving, mud-sliding river otter.

At the moment a sleek female otter is in pursuit of a channel catfish. Chasing the fish by land is more fun and much more sporting. When the doomed catfish heads for deep water, the real chase begins. The otter will plunge into the water, giving the fish a head start, catch up with it and quickly capture her prey.

Suddenly the otter stops and turns her head as though she is being followed. Sure enough, bounding through the reeds, tripping and stumbling as they go, are two bright-eyed otter pups that are just beginning to learn the reckless ways of their breed.

The noonday sun moves quickly past its zenith and the shadows lengthen as the sunlight grazes the treetops. Nightfall, and a silent, watchful bird of the night stands motionless in the reeds. Bright red eyes gleam in the dark. With the caution of a midnight thief the black-crowned night heron stalks its prey. Pygmy killifish and mudminnows swarm in the narrows of the channel and more bright red eyes glow in the dark.

A pig frog croaks a flawless duet with a barking tree frog. Frogs that click, frogs that peep and frogs that grunt join the chorus of hooting owls and chirping katydids. The night sounds are deafening.

A hungry alligator roars and the swamp is silenced, but only for a moment. The sky is filled with the rush of wings and the squawks of fleeing herons as they take to the safety of the treetops. Then all is quiet until a daring pig frog croaks a singular note and is answered from a distance by the hoot of an owl.

Thin sheets of crystal-clear ice cling to the shadow side of the quiet cove. The night has been cold and the alligators remain on the river bottom. A flock of white ibises gathers on the branches of a cypress tree, awaiting the first rays of the morning sun. The most common of the swamp birds, they roost in the densely wooded areas of the swamp, but their feeding grounds are quite often many miles away.

Each morning the ibises rise in huge white flocks and make their journey to the distant "prairies." There they spend the day probing the shallow water for crayfish and snails.

The sun climbs higher, melting the thin ice. The alligators rise to the surface as the warm rays of the sun bring life back to the swamp. Flying low on the horizon, like a string of white pearls, the ibises disappear from sight.

The channel to Minnie's Lake is winding, dark and festooned with Spanish moss. Some of the passageways are barely wide enough to allow a small boat to squeeze through. Oftentimes the channel disappears into a solid mass of moss and tangled branches. The temptation is strong to turn back, but once again there is a break in the wall of green and the apprehensive traveler pushes forward. Strange sounds come from the forest, the eerie effects of invisible occupants preoccupied with survival.

An otter crashes through the underbrush as the shriek of an unknown bird fills the air. The ever-present alligator keeps a sharp watch from the dense growth of pickerelweed and neverwets, and a cottonmouth snake suns himself on a fallen log. Patches of sunlight pierce the deep shadows, and a prothonotary warbler catches a light beam that reveals him in full song. Minnie's Lake is still miles away.

Upstream, against the slow but steady current, the channel gets darker and gloomier, as the overhanging branches become more heavily laden with Spanish moss. No sunlight penetrates the thick foliage. Swamp bats flit through the trees and raccoons slink back into the shadows of the midday twilight. The silence is disconcerting. Tales of phantoms and ghosts creep into the mind. Something big and rough brushes the bottom of the boat. A sunken log? An alligator?

Standing quietly amidst the trunks of cypress trees, a common egret is poised to strike. Somewhere in the swamp her hungry fledglings await her return.

A cloud moves slowly in front of the sun. The silvery tips of the Spanish moss are touched by a gentle breeze as the swamp grows darker still, but the channel is too narrow for the traveler to turn and flee.

31

From the treetops come the squawks of young egrets. Huddled together, in a poorly constructed nest of twigs and branches, are three scrawny birds waiting to be fed. The mother lands on the nest with a crop full of half-digested fish, regurgitates and stuffs the food down the fledglings' throats. It is hard to believe that these ugly young birds will grow to be as graceful and as beautiful as the delicate white bird that is feeding them. A wood stork croaks a warning and silence returns to the swamp.

The pungent smell of swamp water, peat moss and rotting vegetation drifts through the air. The wary egret has flown away and in her place stands the "Captain of the Guard," the curious and ever-watchful wood stork.

The sun breaks through the clouds, dispelling the hypnotic gloom. In an instant Okefenokee becomes a magic emerald forest. The trees come alive with bird song; butterflies come out of hiding and the dark brown waters are flecked with gold.

An old alligator, floating half submerged in the channel, suddenly springs to life, and with the speed of a torpedo gives chase. The chase is brief and the alligator catches the catfish completely by surprise.

Okefenokee is a breeding ground for the American alligator. During the mating season the dark hours of the swamp are filled with the roars and bellows of the courting reptiles. The female lays up to sixty eggs and then covers them in a mound of mud and grass. For months she will remain

nearby until she hears tiny, hungry growls coming from the mound. She then will uncover her brood and lead them to the water.

Alligators will eat anything that moves and that includes each other. They grow about a foot each year until they are six feet long, then more slowly, some of them reaching fifteen feet in length.

The afternoon is hot. The sun sparkles on the honey-colored water and another harmless-looking "log" floats gently down the stream.

In a shady cove, where the water hardly moves and the maiden-cane grows tall, there is a tender courtship taking place. A handsome black-and-white bird raises and lowers his fanlike crest while uttering soft sounds. An unconcerned grayish-brown female is the object of his performance.

The elegant hooded merganser flutters in zigzag circles around the totally indifferent female. He perches briefly on a fallen branch, puffs his chest and makes a spectacular dive into the water. Surely his would-be mate will notice him now!

The female pretends to ignore his presence, but ever so slowly she swims to his side. When the courtship ends, the pair will find, high above the waterline, a hollow tree in which the female will lay her eggs. In a few weeks the shy merganser will become a fierce and protective mother of her brood. But for now, the courtship continues as the male makes another spectacular dive.

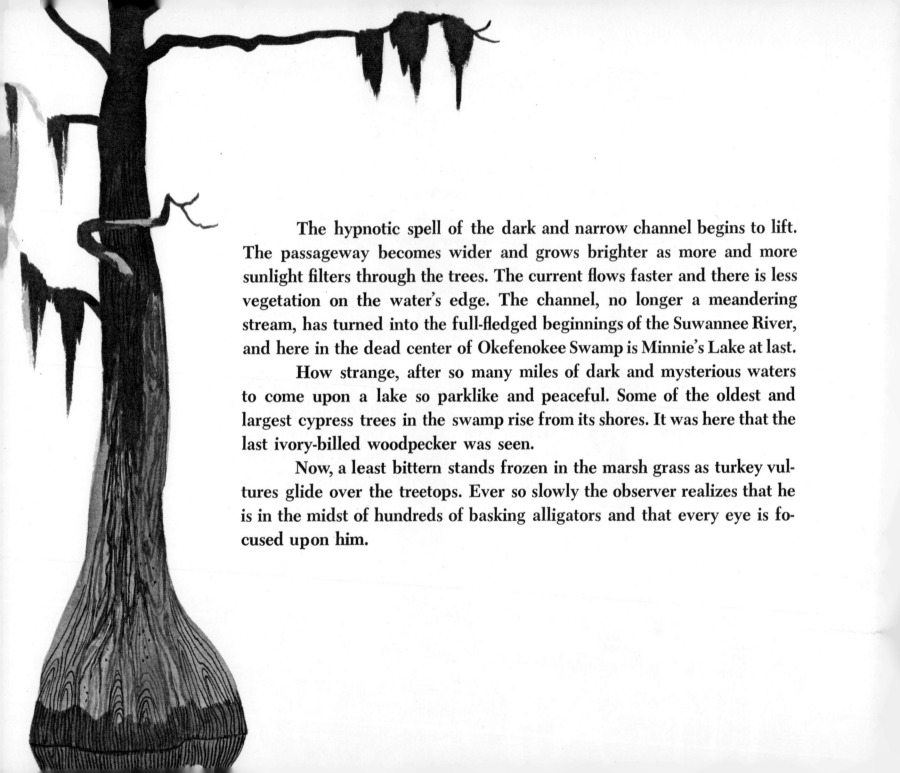

The hypnotic spell of the dark and narrow channel begins to lift. The passageway becomes wider and grows brighter as more and more sunlight filters through the trees. The current flows faster and there is less vegetation on the water's edge. The channel, no longer a meandering stream, has turned into the full-fledged beginnings of the Suwannee River, and here in the dead center of Okefenokee Swamp is Minnie's Lake at last.

How strange, after so many miles of dark and mysterious waters to come upon a lake so parklike and peaceful. Some of the oldest and largest cypress trees in the swamp rise from its shores. It was here that the last ivory-billed woodpecker was seen.

Now, a least bittern stands frozen in the marsh grass as turkey vultures glide over the treetops. Ever so slowly the observer realizes that he is in the midst of hundreds of basking alligators and that every eye is focused upon him.

At Minnie's Lake there is a bird that walks on lily pads and spatterdock as though on dry land. He bobs and weaves, darts and dashes and barely gets his feet wet. Sometimes he cackles and scurries like a chicken and sometimes he swims like a duck. His long green legs and slender toes make it easy for him to climb bushes as well as to skip across the lily pads. He is hunting constantly for aquatic insects and plant lice.

The purple gallinule is as brave as he is handsome for he will on occasion walk right over the back of a sleeping alligator. The gallinule disappears in a clump of marsh marigold and his soft cackle now comes from the reeds. The setting sun warns that it is time to make haste. There are three hours of daylight remaining and it is wise to be gone by dark.

Daybreak. A pier juts from the black waters of Billy's Island. It seems out of place in the early morning mist. The eerie feeling that lingers in the swamp is strongest here, on the most solid piece of land in Okefenokee. It was on this island that the most serious attempt to conquer the swamp was made—and failed. Only the silent trees bear witness to the total defeat of those men who came to haul the cypress away. Exploitation, fire, deluge and drought—each in its turn has failed to lay waste the Okefenokee.

The lumbering town is gone. Slash pine and wild magnolia grow from its flimsy foundations. Bobcats roam freely where children once played. The steam boiler of an abandoned locomotive has long since rusted into the ground and the railroad tracks lie buried forever in the sandy soil. Nothing remains but the ghost of Billy Bowlegs, the Seminole chief who once lived on the island.

The towering loblolly pines that were planted so carefully by Daniel Lee stir in the morning breeze as they whisper a wind song to the people of another time.

The wild creatures of the forest have reclaimed Billy's Island. White-tailed deer wander in the pinelands and wild turkeys hide in the sawtoothed palmettos. Some of the trees wear the scars of the bears that have returned, the claw marks on some of the pines reaching as high as seven feet. Perhaps they are reminders that the island really belongs to all the wild creatures that live there.

The quiet solitude of the island is broken by the noisy appearance of a blue jay. A large bear lumbers through the palmettos and hesitates for a moment, deciding whether a hornets' nest is worth tearing apart. Being the wise bear that she is, she lowers her head and searches for grubs instead. A Carolina wren sings from the swamp fetterbush and the blue jay pecks at the grubs that the bear has left behind.

45

A full moon casts short, sharp shadows across the thick bed of pine needles that lies on the forest floor. A bobcat slinks from shadow to shadow. Down by the shore a water rat nibbles on a magnolia seedpod, unaware of the stalking predator. The rat scurries over the dry leaves looking for more seedpods and the bobcat follows like a silent, gray ghost.

It is almost too late for the rat when those flashing yellow eyes leap from the dark. With a frenzied squeal the rat makes a dash for the water as the bobcat leaps and misses. The rat seems to run in all directions at once, through piles of leaves, around and around the trees with the snarling, pouncing bobcat close behind. A startled night heron flees from the reeds, screeching in its flight. For a moment the bobcat is confused, and in that brief moment of good fortune the rat disappears into the water. The bobcat twitches her tail, flicks her ears and slinks back into the shadows of the pines.

A familiar-looking fowl pokes his head through the palmetto fronds. He is alert and cautious. Legend has it that a wild turkey can hear a hunter gulp at fifty feet and be gone as quick as a wink. When pursued, wild turkeys race along the ground at breakneck speed, then suddenly explode into the air.

At one time wild turkeys roamed all the eastern forests but today they survive mainly in the slash pine groves of the Deep South. Billy's Island is their sanctuary but they are not without enemies. In the shadows lurks an age-old hunter of young gobblers and old hens, the bobcat.

When nightfall comes, the turkeys roost high in the treetops, safe from the prowling bobcats but exposed to the silent wings of the hungry owls.

The night is still and the moon reveals the silhouettes of six wild turkeys perched on the limb of a loblolly pine.

East of Bugaboo Island and north of Buzzard Roost Lake, Okefenokee becomes a vast expanse of water called the prairies. The dark and haunting channels surrender to the sunlight and the shade-loving plants give way to the carnivorous sundew, the fly-eating pitcher plant and the pennywort.

Small islands of cypress linger on the horizon and the sky yields hordes of birds in flight. Periodically, clumps of peat moss and mud rise from the swamp bottom to become hosts to the wandering, windblown seeds. In time, flowers will bloom on these floating peat bogs. Grass will grow and seedlings will become saplings. When the Indians first stepped on these quaking islands, they saw immense trees tremble and shake and the swamp became known as Oua-qua-pheno-gaw, land of the trembling earth.

The prairies give sanctuary to thousands of waterfowl. When the spring rains fall, the rising water table is the signal for the herons to build new rookeries or to restore the old ones. When the time comes for the fledglings to leave the nest, the waters of the prairies are brimful of fingerlings and frogs. Oua-qua-pheno-gaw has fulfilled her promise to provide.

The tall grasses bend as a soft wind from the south turns the prairie into a sea of golden-brown waves. A sharp gust sends tiny ripples dashing across the cove, rocking the lily pads and whipping the plumes of marsh grass into a frenzy.

A large gray hawk is blown about by the summer breeze. It hovers briefly over a patch of tickweed, then suddenly plunges into the grass and is gone from sight. The shrill call of another hawk pierces the air, and a pair of marsh harriers are on their never-ending search for food.

Flying low over the marsh, they flush out rice rats and mice from their hiding places, then make acrobatic dives into the grass as they give chase to their prey. Somewhere in the prairie is a nest built close to the ground. In it are two downy young harriers, their sharp eyes raised to the sky, awaiting the return of their parents.

The warm wind blows throughout the day, twisting and twirling the long grass, twisting and twirling the gray birds as they hover, flutter and dive.

53

The sounds of cackles, whistles, chuckles and squawks come from the quivering reeds. Black wings and green feet slap, dash and flap across the water as a flock of coots bursts from the edge of the pond. They run pell-mell through the lily pads and flop back into the water. They rise again, like a small dark cloud with dangling green feet, and dash back to where they started. Some dive beneath the surface of the water; others try to dive and discover they don't know how, while still others crash headlong into the reeds.

The American coots behave as though they have no brains in their heads. They gossip, frolic and splash all day long. The fat, happy "mud hens" build frightful-looking nests in which they lay beautiful, speckled brown eggs. As soon as the eggs hatch, the chicks leap into the water. Day after day they tumble from the nest. It is impossible for the hen to look after them because she is too busy hatching the rest of the eggs. The dutiful father does his best to rear the young, but that alone could drive a coot crazy.

A hurricane has spent itself north of Okefenokee Swamp and blown itself out to sea. In its wake lie fallen trees, broken branches and flooded islands of cypress. The raging wind that ripped through the Spanish moss and flattened the marsh grass brought with it two handsome visitors from the savannahs of the tropics.

A pair of swallow-tailed kites were blown north with the summer storm. Beneath the hot August sun they make fantastic swoops and dives with the grace and speed of swallows. Suddenly they fold their wings and plummet toward the earth like falling stars, merely to skim the waters of the prairies or to capture an unsuspecting snake. Up they go again, disappearing from sight, feeding on the wing. They have been known to hover over a forest fire catching the insects that escape the flames.

Truly, the swallow-tailed kites are birds of the air and their joy of flight is halted only by the approaching night.

The season of wind and rain has fallen upon Okefenokee. Gray autumn clouds move swiftly across the November sky, bringing with them the first wave of migrating waterfowl. Green-winged teal and hooded mergansers have left the solitude of Minnie's Lake to gather in the coves of the prairies. The tall grasses have turned brown, their feathery seedpods blown about by the autumn wind.

A solitary egret lingers in the marsh until the approaching winter forbids him to remain. Alligators sink to the bottom of their "holes" to await the warmth of another April.

Each passing day brings more birds from the North. Cypress needles turn from green to orange and then to brown. They drop from the tips of the limbs, leaving the branches bare except for a blanket of Spanish moss. The golden days of autumn will be gone too soon, as suddenly as the reflections in the still black water are shattered by a kingfisher's dive.

A few moments of daylight remain in the evening sky. The chill of the coming winter hangs over the prairies. Silent white ibises are silhouetted across the face of the fading sun on their journey back to Billy's Island. A pair of sandhill cranes stand motionless in the twilight. In a moment they too will be gone. No more sounds of insects or frogs fill the air; even the coots are quiet. In the long weeks ahead Okefenokee Swamp will slumber away the sometimes gentle winter. Frost and ice may still its waters. Cold wind will rattle through the stiff reeds and the summer sounds will seem like a haunting dream.

The cypress trees stand rigid against the stark horizon. The lily pads have withered and the swallow-tailed kites have flown away. The winter constellations shine brightly as darkness falls. Cassiopeia and Orion return to their cold vigil over the black waters of the Okefenokee. The only sounds that the winter night will yield are the creak of a cypress tree and the hoot of a lonely owl.